T0147811

In a Quiet Moment

POEMS

Mary Elizabeth Lee

iUniverse®
Editor's Choice

IN A QUIET MOMENT
POEMS

iUniverse books may be ordered through booksellers or by contacting:

iUniverse
1663 Liberty Drive
Bloomington, IN 47403
www.iuniverse.com
1-800-Authors (1-800-288-4677)

*Because of the dynamic nature of the internet, any web addresses or links contained in
this book may have changed since publication and may no longer be valid. The views
expressed in this work are solely those of the author and do not necessarily reflect the views
of the publisher, and the publisher hereby disclaims any responsibility for them.*

*Any people depicted in stock imagery provided by Getty Images are models,
and such images are being used for illustrative purposes only.
Certain stock imagery © Getty Images.*

ISBN: 978-1-5320-4985-9 (sc)
ISBN: 978-1-5320-4984-2 (e)

Library of Congress Control Number: 2018906937

Print information available on the last page.

iUniverse rev. date: 07/16/2018

For my love

Contents

What Goes Up

When he says, "Not just now.
I am busy," she just looks away.
As he piddles and pretends at cooking,
he may call for the "doodad,"
the "thingamajig," or the "whatchamacallit."
She ignores him most
of the time. When she is
inquisitive and asks him
questions when he is driving
about the construction of the roadway,
he quips, "Jump out and take
a closer look. I will slow down."
He often says when she scolds him,
"You put a bugaboo on me!"
To which she quietly replies,
"You silly bird!" He calls
her his resident scholar, until
she jumps on his back and
rides him a-bug-hunting.

A Step Too Far

Most days she feels like a cauldron
spewing sparks and steam out her rim.
The boil starts deep in her core, no caution

inching up hour by hour, sliding
between her lips like a low belch.
The hot liquid rolls, widening

the tumble out of the opening,
tainting the air. The cauldron
inside her boils, hot water ruining

the calm water with a raging fire.
The hot water spits and splatters
down the side of the pot, a pyre

with a white cloud of stifling steam.
The smell of the burning coals
under the pot becomes a rancid dream.

The water boils away, leaving a residue
sticky and hard at the bottom. The rim
cools during the day as the leftover blows,

dried and flaked, and days later, only a cup
full of flaky clouds at the bottom remains.

Its Very Best

In late summer a lily stays.
Its beauty is more than kind praise.
The view sent me away blessed.
Nature daily sends its very best.

As night blended into view,
I turned from my planned debut.
Heavy darkness blocked the rest.
Nature daily sends its very best.

When winter cold joins us in vain,
the lily crumples, and dying it feigns,
leaving only a leaf pressed.
Nature daily sends its very best.

Only the green sprouts of flower
brighten the spirits with pure power.
Lilies answer the call to express.
Nature daily sends its very best.

Slow Saturday

The library of books darkens
as the sky clouds up for more rain.
Nonthreatening thunder rumbles
like angels moving furniture in heaven.
This day is a day of rest where
I do what I want to do, when I want.

I like to think I have the freedom to want
to write on the weekends before the night darkens
this day as a day of play or where
the sky clouds up for rain.
I have no interest in checking the attic
as the thunder grows farther away in sound.

The day has progressed as I sound
the balance of time between what I want
to do and the thoughts of the attic.
Early morning I eat a bowl of bran flakes, and the sky darkens
before a cup of tea as I read the newspaper before the rain.
The radio sends out bluesy sounds where

its morning listeners go about their business and where
we meet in the grocery store line and shop without talk.
The sky pauses and only sprinkles a few drops of rain—
a blessing for many who had planned their day's wants
and feared further complications when cleaning up the darkness
of the memories of their safety in their attics.

The sunny afternoon brings to mind the hot attic
where the water heater stopped heating water
when temperatures became too hot but occasioned no spirit darkening.
The rain clouds for the day have moved away with their thunder,
and the afternoon becomes more of what I want
with the sky clearing of clouds, leaving no thoughts of rain.

We listen to special reports and hear no more about rain.
Relax! Ignore the warning from the hot attic.
A good time to do what I want to do, when I want—
this day is to be a day of rest and reading of poetry, where
no alarm from the water heater is to be heard.
But again the library and my mood have darkened.

The house is getting hot without more rain. No sounds or cool air from the attic! The air-conditioning has quit blowing cool air. How I want to enjoy the weekend and read!

The Gentle Wind

Zephyrus, send a soft wing
to cool this hot spring.
A soft breeze from the west—
let it be light and royal—
is what I call the best.
Let it be gentle and only
rustle the leaves of the flowers.
Bend the small saplings firmly.
Polish the buds before the shower.
Pass your wings across
my brow, letting them
faintly feel like moss.
Zephyrus, be the gentle wind,
a gentle wind well defined.

Training for the Hunter

The bird chatter grew louder
and more instructive. Two Harris
hawks, the falconer's choice,
stood on the limb of the red oak tree.
One flew to a nearby oak and continued
calling to the younger hawk, dancing side to side
on the limb, restrained only by the uncertainty
of his wings. As the shrill screeching
grew louder, the young one gained his courage,
flaunted his skills, and leaned into the wind.
With imagined skill he flew straight over
to the waiting hawk. The parent lowered
praise in shrill chirps on the young one
for being so brave and flying so straight.
Off the parent and the young hawk flew
together to learn more about hunting.

In the Moonlight

Instead of gazing at the sea
the way she does on other nights,
the moon looks down on Avenida
Copacabana at the sights.[1]

Instead of gazing at the sea,
the moon looks down on BR Walden Free
with a sheet of yellow flowing over the houses built
close to shore where the cypress stand to fight the silt.
The trees reign as the moon's companions-to-be.
Instead of gazing at the sea

the way the trees do on other nights,
the trees like careful parents make sure all is right.
Their massive trunks wade in the water
without fear and happy to saunter,
keeping the picture perfect for the moon so bright,
the way they do on other nights.

The moon looks down on Avenida
and BR's Walden equally ace *vivida*.
The water lilies residing in the lake,
their faces turned upward for their sake
to make up the audience *de la comandita*.[2]
The moon looks down on Avenida

Copacabana at the sights
to thrill the tourists under the city lights.
The Walden Pond soothes its suitors,
enjoying the moonlight with their viewers.
Celebrate BR Walden and celebrate moonlight,
Copacabana at the sights.

---

[1] From Elizabeth Bishop's "Going to the Bakery."
[2] The translation of this is "of the partnership."

Protest Day

These unpurged images of day recede;
The Emperor's drunken soldiers are abed;
Night resonance receded, night-walkers' song
After great cathedral gong.[3]

The unpurged images of day recede.
All are unhappy and fear the needs
of the people, while the dominant culture
is quick to declare the oppressed vultures.
A time to reconcile, fight, or concede.
The unpurged images of day recede.

The emperor's drunken soldiers are abed
and do not bring the issue to a head.
What will result for us all
will determine whether we live or fall.
The nation must answer the cries of the dead.
The emperor's drunken soldiers are abed.

Night resonance receded, the nightwalkers' song
fills the night and comforts the wronged.
The protests continue throughout the days
while no one is changing his ways.
Each holds the belief that they deserve the throne.
Night resonance receded, nightwalkers' song.

After the great cathedral gong,
marchers continue with their song,
marching and singing, feeling their power.
Others seem to feel the event's gone sour.
Who will heal the wronged
after the great cathedral gong?

---

[3] From W. B. Yeats's "Byzantium."

The Art of Waiting

As the soft sounds of the radio from the nearby room float near,
the air from the vents brings cool waves into the room.

I do not know the details of your arrival. I do know
that you said during a phone call that you were coming today.

Waiting is so hard for me to do, and I have a hard time
squeezing the hours of the day into the vise of meaning.

Dressed comfortably in black jeans and a plaid shirt, I wait
as the sun moves to the west, sending more warmth into the room.

A trip to the grocery store for milk, bread, and butter will use up
a cartridge of time. My heart flutters at the possibility of your visit.

I sit here rereading the newspaper as my thoughts float away.
A visit to the local grill will be a nice opportunity for a visit.

The soothing music continues to float through the room from the radio
and circles me in happiness, causing me for a moment to forget the vigil.

I hear the rumble of your car's motor in the driveway.
Frustration disappears. You are home once again!

Search for Meaning

You say I look really good.
I am surprised that you do not
see the fraying around my edges
like that of the tattered toy rabbit
in another story. I still stand tall
like the old magnolia at the edge
of the property, with its rough
enlarged bark midway on the trunk.
The tree boasts a scar from some injury or
invasion that covers a part of her body.
She still thrills others with her big waxy
leaves and white blooms. Each spring
she dresses herself for the spring
parade and continues to sprout
new growth, still giving. I escape
these thoughts to stand beside
the decaying tree in Van Gogh's
Starry Night on the pathway to the hamlet below.
This stripping away of leaves and
splintering of trunk is the natural design,
a change that I wait to see when I too
sprout a new bonnet of leaves
and grow a new frock of bark, ready
to support the march in the spring parade.

Quiet Trait

Bold courage
lies quietly in the
chests of a few—waiting.

Not found in
learned holy halls
of churches or colleges.

Ballooning,
it surprises the hero
too, when courage soars skyward.

Overwhelm
the physical over thought
when there is danger.

Praise freely brave souls who save
the moment by saving another.

So What!

So what if my hand is easily held.
So what if I upset your apple cart.
So what if I am not easily quelled.
Still,
hold me close to your heart.
So what if I'm neither bleached nor gray.
So what if I tease and taunt with boos.
So what if a mean spirit haunts my days.
Still,
you should understand my news.
This poem may not find its way,
but I must not give up in dismay.

After the Flood

Debris from the flood was not expected where
there were soiled carpets. Baseboards were piled high
with trim, with flooring, furniture, and Sheetrock there.

Structures remain with the repairs inside,
still unfinished. There is nothing left
but bare ribs of structures to guide.

Enough for some to begin the repairs;
for others, there is no hope that remains,
the sunken ship too deep to rescue on a dare,

too much to buy to cover with calm ease
the ribs and to finish the floors. Too much
for weary hearts to fathom in high seas.

Left for others to complete; community pain
remains with no one familiar
to talk with down the lane.

It will require many years of hard work
to make familiar living structures perk.

The Saga of Waiting

The day I wait for someone special to arrive is a day spent in excitement. I awake early and get the house ready for my visitors. I do not have much cleaning to do: straighten the fringe on the area rugs, empty the waste cans, and pick up lost clothing or magazines. These tasks will not take long. I wish I had more to clean. It would keep me busy.

The day I wait is
a day to fix and spruce.
Tasks fail to keep me.

It is nearing 12:00 noon with the soft sounds of the radio from the nearby room floating in. The air-conditioned air feels so cool and good on this hot day. A walk outside reveals the blooming red, purple, and pink crepe myrtles. The daylilies are in full orange dress, and the irises have come dressed in dark purple. The blooms on the satsuma are gone, but the buds of fruit have started.

Nature's blooms are everywhere.
Daylilies circle cannas,
a bouquet of red.

I make a trip to Robert's for bread, milk, and ground meat. A stroganoff would be a good dish to fix. I could make spaghetti. Guests always enjoy having cooked food when they arrive around noon. Tea, green salad, and a soft french bread will complete the dinner. I should get busy and make the dish now. I settle on spaghetti and meatballs.

The grocery store
displays wine, bread, food, and plants,
a fine selection.

Back home, the soothing music continues to float around the room from the radio, soothing me. It is nearing the hour of arrival. I fuss over the food and keep a piqued ear for the car in the driveway. I think I hear the motor of the car. I must look to see if it is them or someone driving around in the cul-de-sac. It is them!

Visitors arrive,
knock gingerly on the front door.
Emotions overtake us.

After the Game

Fans cheered to see the winning coach.
Slowly they departed from the bleachers.
They wanted to see the new coach up close.

Fans wanted to hang around for some talk.
They wanted to hear what Coach had to say about the game.
They wanted to know the players' deft walk.

Some fans headed for the players' locker room.
Others stood aimlessly on the empty field.
Only reporters went into the locker room.

The new coach concentrated on the players,
eager to hug them as they hugged him,
staff still happy with the friendly favors.

Coach and pleased players agreed on a team oath
with the calm players circling their winning coach.
The binding agreement was pleasing to both.

The game was the first big win for the football year.
Coach and players proved it to pleased peers.

All's Fair in Expanding World

In vast seas of dark matter
and hot gas, these hermits reside.
These behemoths are bloated
from devouring their neighbors.
Large ones consume smaller ones
through violent gusts of gravity,
leaving luminous shards along
their paths like an airplane broken up
in flight. The universe is filled
with disembodied streams of stars,
gas, and dust, ghostly remains
of once normal galaxies. Like a
cannibal as it grows larger, its increased
gravity makes grabbing new victims easier.
It means survival of the largest is the rule.
The surviving nuclei of those stripped
masquerade as globular clusters. Our
hermit is the Milky Way. It takes
the substance of smaller galaxies
like a schoolyard bully taking lunch
money or like taffy being pulled apart
before being devoured. It can add a billion
new stars to our home galaxy, the Milky Way.
In vast seas of dark matter and hot gas
beyond the naked eye, large hermits
look for smaller ones to devour. As powerful
telescopes show us, the Milky Way's presence
as it is known today is temporary because
it is not the largest in the vast sea of dark matter
and gases.

Along the Road

In the fields along the road, the vetch
glistens under the coverlet of dew.
The beads of sky-blue glass peeking
out are luminous but reveal only a few.

As the morning sun dries up the dew,
it leaves the vetch again in its green heaven.
Five cows are in the field, only a grazing few.

The light of day passes, and night comes.
Tomorrow's sun and dew will be the sum.

Arriving at Truth

The storm pit, his safe spot
built several years earlier,
protected from twisters.
The smell of the earth floor
permeates the air, as does the strong
smell of the ten-by-twelve creosote posts
along the sides and back that stand
against the winds.

I remember the times
I sought him out to hear
his wisdom. He shared his truth,
spreading it like peanut butter
on bread, sticking his comments
together with the honey in his voice.
I possessed clarity when I left him.

Wisdom comes from measuring
knowledge against experience.
Quiet and time alone encourage
this achievement. Thinking through
the problems of working a farm
ensured the seer's wisdom.

With Purpose

A night without the moon
is a lonely one in June.
Its birth from a colliding mass
fast with Earth's lagoons
reveals mysteries that pass
in her efforts to swoon.
She spreads its light,
showing herself
on a cloudless night
as a full moon self.
Given her optimal fullness in the sky,
my heart soars with romance,
with my lover as my ally.
So romantic is the moon
on a dark night in this cocoon.

Birthday Dinner

Slow this dark night down for the jeweled town.
The darkness hovered and covered quickly.
Nothing was so important to stop frowns.
The guests must be dressed and pretty.

The attendants were ready then to start,
dressed for the party and the gala dinner.
They dared not bring out their motley charts.

The guest elegantly dressed appeared.
The pleased ones greeted her with roaring cheers.

Nature's Caretaker

A year later, summer is hot,
but the cannas, daisies, and pink
and coral dahlias
continue their work,
blooming happily.

Rosy purple daisy flowers
and purple asters show
their new colors. Midnight
and Firebird trumpet-shaped
flowers dance in the breezes.

The chirping birds swoop
and dart, but the woman
who celebrated them
and summer flowers is no
longer here. She knew them all.

She slipped away early one morning.
No one can replace her, but
the flowers and birds remember
and celebrate the caretaker daily
with songs and displays of beauty.

Christmas Bells

In remembrance of Edgar Allen Poe

Good to hear bells,
bells, bells, bells. Bells ringing around
everywhere. I love to hear up close
rhyming, chiming prose
on Christmas Day with the brass bells
at churches' doors,
rolling and tolling.
The swinging and the ringing of
the bells rime until midnight like doves cooing.
A soft sound provides good timing.
Across the dale,
jingling bells swell.

Christmas Moments

Steam rises up
from the iron pot on the trivet,
announcing welcome teatime.
Squares of repeat chime
in sweet chocolate,
stroke warm frolic.
Steaming cups of hot chocolate
please the guests and warm their thoughts
as the guests enjoy the holiday.
Mailboxes stacked with cards in lots,
framed in a tree of cups,
a mesmerizing setup.

Clever One

Second youngest boy of eleven,
he always knew how to share.
He was clever at reading lips,
so being deaf did not keep him
from knowing what was being said.
He felt a closeness with his eldest
sister and often drove hundreds of miles
to visit her, enjoying the visits
with other family members. He often
took his niece to stay with his sister
for the summer. He supported himself
cutting pulpwood, and retired when
he was worn out, only to start a garden
that produced more than he or his
neighbors could use. His life spent
cutting pulpwood rendered his body
pained from arthritis, but he keeps
a smile on his lips and kind words
on his fingertips.

Crossed T's

I often straddled a broomstick
when I was very young, and I
would head over the hills of shimmering
crystals through the valleys of beaded
memories, but never going too far
from home. Now I have learned
from my years to straddle a wild thought,
with a strong hand to tame it,
grasping it around the throat
until I teach it to grow
into a bouquet of calm moments.
Without great care, the undercurrents
from jealous thoughts cause such waves
of strong winds that they buck the rider
or knock the rider off under a low-lying insult.
It takes cartons of courage to train
new thoughts to be tame enough
to be ridden through the continent
of challenges and to be sailed
over oceans of lemongrass
in search of a new adventure.

Dude, Plow Horse

Waves of early-
morning coolness
melt against
the warm ground.
The stinging nettles
grow thick in the grasses,
stabbing the legs with pain,
but no sign of the plow horse.

The years had moved
along a wide tunnel
of memories through which
I passed each day, reworking
the content of many blinded
to their original moments.
I felt sadness that day because
we found the horse dead of old age.

I seem to be caught
in the tangle of memories,
remembering a farmer's belief
that lets animals live out their lives
on the farm, never to be sold for soap.
An honorable man was he!

Early-Morning Coolness

The dew sits like shimmering crystals,
sparkling in the coolness of the morning
as the sun rises in the sky. The robins and
bluebirds sing and dance in midair.
The sparrows and blue jays watch as robins and
bluebirds entertain from nearby trees. The fragrance
from the blooms nearby with natural essences
of citrus, apple, and cherry blend together
with a hint of precious sandalwood and
vanilla musk in the air. This kingdom
stands like bushes, one for robins, one
for bluebirds, one for sparrows, one for blue jays,
one for reptiles, another for primates, including
us, and many bushes for plants enjoying
the coolness of the morning. As the sun rises in the sky,
all join in the singing as the morning yawns a wave
of coolness before the heat consumes the day.

Election Time

The study grows much darker as the clouds thicken for rain.
The radio voices are the only companions in this political fog.

Beyond this screen it is too dark to read or to write.
Only the low hum of the radio breaks the silence.

The warmth of my jacket protects me from the spirits
coming from the air-conditioning that always give me a chill.

The primary election talk spews from the airways, interrupting.
I grow tired of the political babble from candidates.

There is an attempt to manufacture news from the candidates,
every comment captured in midair.

Every pundit wants to comment on the candidate who has made
the most ridiculous statements about gender or race.

I hope that this talk will move us to the selection of a reputable
candidate who can unite us after this dance of vitriol.

Faith and Love

She did not think about the hot, grainy,
sticky sand in her sandals
or the sweat streaming down her
face from her dark hair. The summer
heat was hard to take because he drew
a crowd wherever he was, always, it seemed,
beyond the shade of a tree. She often prayed
for a shower of rain to cool her body
in the loose-fitting robes. But how she
feared for him. His words riled
the rulers, and there would be
his life to pay if they turned against him.
She adjusted her duties to stand
beside him, subjecting herself
to possible prosecution. She had
stepped off the page into the religiosity
of the world, ignoring the desert heat and
the hot sand between her toes. She was
often his better half when they retired
from view. True, some of the young
women were jealous of their
relationship. The heat and the sand
she forgave when she thought
of the importance of her hero. She shielded
herself through her faith from the angry
taunts thrown at her when others
thought her position beside him
too special, but she knew him and
loved him well as her lover.

She could mediate the divine,
greater than the Gospels tell,
greater than the church. Why else
was she there to clean and wash
his body when the unimaginable
occurred? Mary Magdalene
was more than we in the West
want to imagine to Jesus,
the Nazarene.

Food for Thought

Travel, trouble, music, art.
A kiss, a frock, a rhyme—
I never said they feed my heart.
But still they pass my time.[4]

Television, radio, stereo.
A look, a whistle, a shout—
I never said this makes a beau,
And they do cause doubt.

Friends, acquaintances, foes.
A hug, a letter, a text—
I would not say they support my shows,
But they do keep the memories vexed.

Husband, relatives, cousins.
A text, a shout, a pain—
I would say the joy of a husband
And love for him remains.

---

[4] From Dorothy Parker's "Faute de Mieux."

From Afar

When the rain falls softly on the tin roof,
The blooms of shrub-trained trees decorate
And blanket the ground, weatherproofed.
I stroke the cat in my soft chair and wait.

From the distance comes the train whistle
Warning traffic of danger,
Sending the rumbling sound
That pleases my ear from afar.

The clouds move on; family's home;
Some eat together, some with the TV ...
Although my niece is gone, I hear these sounds,
When the rain falls softly on the tin roof.

Full of Energy

She became a ball of excitement
at the sound of music, bouncing
around the room, tapping her foot
and clapping her hands to the beat and
swinging her hips in dance. She relished
visits from family. Her energy would
sweep across the room, melting into hugs
and kisses. She was a seamstress during
her work life. She was generous with her
sewing skills, making quilts, coverlets,
and dresses for anyone who needed
them. She loved crafts and made pretty
boxes and pieces of jewelry for anyone lucky
enough to receive them. Later in life, she
spent her time playing games with her
friends in the nursing home. A visit would
unleash the energy from her eyes and the radiance
of her smile that would make you forget she
had been deaf since birth.

Gifts for All

Shoppers drop coins
for the less fortunate into the bucket.
Inside, shopkeepers push sales pell-mell
with the tinkles and the chiming of the bells.
In rising rhythm during long days,
children play with bells
ringing on shined shoes.
All joining together,
happy to forget the weather,
dancing to a happy symphony.
Calling to join,
chiming adjoins.

Flood in August

If it shines or if it rains,
Little will I care or know.
Days, like drops upon a pane,
Slip, and join, and go.[5]

If it shines or if it rains,
I can only say, I disdain
Nature's overflow of bayous and creeks
That has wrecked the homes of the meek.
How can the people stand the pain?
If it shines or if it rains,

Little will I care or know,
Some might say. I wish them only one row to hoe.
The damage rests on tired backs
Where stacks of sand in sacks
Could not hold back what they would owe.
Little will I care or know?

Days, like drops upon a pane,
Leave a debt like a ball and chain.
The courage needed to rebuild,
So hard for the elderly and the unskilled.
We dare not say they should be ashamed.
Days, like drops upon a pane,

Slip, and join, and go.
And what about their payments to escrow?
How will people come to reign
Again and know they are safe in this plain?
Experts recommend organizing with their neighbors: forgo,
Slip, and join, and go.

---

[5] From Dorothy Parker's "The New Love."

Gravitational Pull

Humorous to see! Two canines
walking two humans, jerking them
this way and that, yelping at cars.
I have seen a child or two with
the same demeanor and purpose
walking the parent this way and that,
pulling and screaming to get their
own way. Yet this is human life,
leading, pulling us in ways
we do not want, like, or need,
much like addictive drugs that
pull us in dark directions and
numb us to life's happenings.
We humans find it hard to handle
those we love and hate. The mind
swirls with anxiety with every
new leaf of life, leaving us spent.
Do not forsake us, Athena and
Minerva! Leave us with the wisdom
we yearn for! Take away the humor
we see when other humans fail.
Humorous to see, that is,
when it's not me!

Gray Day

This gray day seemed lonely,
even with family.
Breezes outside stumbled
and rolled without notice.
Cheerful conversations—
cheerful conversations
lapped around the buzzing
room, but did not remove
the dark cloud settling now
over me this warm night.

Helen of Troy

She only came for a short stay,
and that was enough to cause
the thirteen-year-old girl to be enthralled.
Her luggage bore the travel stamps
of exotic places. Her gowns of lace
and chiffon were enough to make
the teenager realize that there was
another world out there that she
would love to sample. The faint smell
of cigarette smoke and perfume lingered
behind this queen as she walked.
She carried her clothes well and
seemed always to be planning
or thinking about something else
or somewhere other than where she was.
Her restlessness and fast talk only piqued
the teenager's interests because
she was feeling restless herself.

Here Comes Santa!

Fake tree on the bar
glistening with lights galore.
The lights at the base skywrite,
bathing the fiber optic tree like pyrite
in happy primary colors.
Colors move,
gliding, rippling.
Artificial art creates joy
that makes way for toys
up the wire limbs to the top.
A toddler squeals, spars.
She's the star!

Disguised Intent

Heresies
fly into brave faces
of the accepted, the established.

These beliefs
feed fears of the prepared
and the unprepared.

Provided
by friends—enemies,
they infect our clear thinking.

Disguising
their intent, they fly
like trained cues into blind truth.

A rare refreshing world it would be
with nothing but clear thinking and truth.

A Place of Love

I went to the Garden of Love,
And saw what I never had seen:
A Chapel was built in the midst,
where I used to play on the green.[6]

I went to the Garden of Love
and visited the house of the clove.
The structure was empty but familiar,
for I had grown up there, similar
to the others I knew to be doves.
I went to the Garden of Love

and saw what I never had seen:
an empty house with no one keen.
The rooms all looked the same,
only no one was there to blame.
I wondered where else I had been
and saw what I never had seen:

a chapel was built in the midst
of the familiar, rounding out the twist
of life that had left me adrift,
to escape what I knew had caused the tiff.
As I turned to go, I saw on the great list
that a chapel was built in the midst

where I used to play on the green.
There, I asked everyone for the scheme
that would explain the world to me.
Only the Ouija board counseled that D
would be my hero in every life scene
where I used to play on the green.

---

6 From William Blake's "The Garden of Love."

His Things

She was cleaning—there is always
that to do—when she found,
at the top of the closet, his old
silk vest. She called me.[7]

She was cleaning—there is always
something to iron or to wash each day.
The need to clean and straighten comes
second nature in this world to some.
The book found nearby contained his lays.
She was cleaning—there is always

that to do—when she found,
at the top of the shelf, a knife bound
in a cloth that brought her thoughts
to the battles that had been fought
like the things left for the hound.
That to do—when she found,

at the top of the closet, his old
gun she thought he had sold.
No one laid claim to the gun
as the group spread out under the sun.
It was a problem often not told.
At the top of the closet, his old

silk vest. She called me.
We joined her, and he,
the older brother, said best
that he would like the vest.
Yes, it was the piece she—
silk vest. She called me.

---

[7] From Tess Gallagher's "Black Silk."

I Seek

I seek—
With a glass of chardonnay to limber my thoughts
With my mom's record player to keep her music alive
With patterns and material to design clothes that flatter
With scissors to cut away superfluous white paper
With friends, good conversations, and good food
With my fingers on the keys of a computer to research
With fringed scarves to train my hair
With rhymes and cadences to please
that are necessary to the rhythm of life
With dyes and stains to correct rotten wood
With books to know much of others
With embroidery to decorate a piece of cloth
With my grandmother's bin to mimic her
With my mom's records to listen to with understanding
With a religion, a past, a present
With quilting squares to make a design
With crafts to keep myself busy
With new ideas, new thoughts
With pets to satisfy my emotional needs
With creative ideas to manage a learning center
With tutors, students, and staff to provide assistance
I've sought needy students!
With love and respect for students' learning
From the depth of my understanding,
I seek, I seek, I seek …
With commitment to enhance the skills of the learner

I Would Think

Travel, trouble, music, art.
A kiss, a frock, a rhyme—
I never said they feed my heart.
But still they pass my time.[8]

Television, radio, stereo.
A look, a whistle, a tune—
I never said this hover pleases.
But it does cause me to be uneasy.

Friends, acquaintances, lovers.
A hug, a letter, an email—
I would not say they thrill me still.
But they do keep the memories real.

Husband, relatives, cousins.
A text, a shout, a bill—
the thrills come in dozens.
But the love never chills.

---

[8] From Dorothy Parker's "Faute de Mieux."

Man in the Moon

He enjoyed sitting on the front porch
in his rocking chair in the coolness
of the evening. The light from the window
behind him and the distant moon were
barely a faint glow on the weeping willow
on his right looking out, with the red begonias
and Joseph's coat lining the porch edge.
On this night his five-year-old
granddaughter joined him in her
rocker beside him. He sat
quietly in his work khakis,
his arms resting on the arms
of the rocker and his big,
dirt-scarred, worn high-tops
crossed. The young child sat
quietly, sensing something
unknown, when the granddad,
clearing his throat, told her
that he would die soon.
"I do not want you to be sad.
See the moon? When you miss me,
look at the moon. That's where
I will be," he said. She slipped
back in the large wooden rocker
and began to rock quietly
in the dim light.

In a Quiet Moment

An idea thought
Fails to inspire
When never sought.

An idea thought,
Sympathy naught,
Static quelled.

An idea only thought
Fails to inspire.

Invitation

An invitation sent
Happily and expectantly.
Lost its intent

An invitation sent
Hard feelings vent
Happiness dissipates

An invitation sent
Happily and expectantly

Flood in October 2016

A rainy week
Flooded homes and businesses
Overflow from bayous and creeks

A rainy week
Owners endure doublespeak
Weeks of misery

A rainy week
Flooded homes and businesses

Flood and Mold

A rainy week
Honorable helpers
The flooded seek

Water stands for weeks
No news midweek
Mold grows

A rainy week
Honorable helpers

Belated Wish

A birthday card
Dropped in grass
Slightly scarred

A birthday card
A thrill for the bard
Party planned

A birthday card
Dropped in grass

Into the Pines

I walked down the driveway by the old home site.
The grass worn away by vehicles was revealing.
I could see behind the house that pine thickets have cropped up,
the lot of land next to the house had been planted, and under them
lay the pine straw under the planted pine trees everywhere.
To get to my special place—eight acres require many footsteps,

but I knew the way well and on the grass-bare ground—I made the steps
on the ground made by the tires that took me by the old clapboard home site,
out the gate, around the barn, and back to the fence line to the pines.
Everywhere the thickets thrived as far as I could see in their greenness revealed.
The pine straw formed a thick brown carpet and was stacked under them,
and the thickets thickened on their own as they matured.

The thickness of the trees had not cropped up
where many years of mowing and planting had kept clean steps.
Still the pines with their long trunks under them
kept the forest floor clean of weeds like a well-kept city site
as if they had sweepers who raked and flattened the straw,
a natural trick that I still respect and love, this covering up.

Having grown up on a small farm, I remember with love
the seedlings of trees and fuchsia flowers on the wild clover that cropped up.
Both had always fascinated me. I loved Nature's revealing
it to me when I followed the footsteps
to the large sweet gum that had become my personal site,
where from under the sweet gum I watched the pines dance to their own music.

A swath of grassland lay between the sweet gum and them
as if the pines had marked their territory, allowing no pines to cross this site
of grass, or allowing no young pines to play in the designated site.
Some oaks had grown naturally, but they had not cropped up
without care. They were designated to the side, a few steps
away. This natural planting by Nature was amazing.

I stood in awe of Nature's plan and the trees' desire to reveal
that their natural thickets stood firm and no other trees grew under them.
The grassland must have been kept through the years by my dad's mowers,
or the trees were more careful of seeding themselves when cropping up.
Pine thickets with oaks on the fence line and one massive sweet gum only up
in one spot kept the memory alive of my special site.

I walked the eight acres back to the home site. What wonderful secrets
Nature reveals—! What if I studied the pattern of trees cropping up and found
them never to seed their babies under our footsteps because they fear being
stomped?

Late Saturday Night

Turning and turning in the widening gyre
The falcon cannot hear the falconer;
Things fall apart; the center cannot hold;
Mere anarchy is loosed upon the world.[9]

Turning and turning in the widening gyre
is the angry spin in conflicting fire,
loosing pent-up anger and distress,
quick to issue actions unblessed.
None of the confused seems to tire.
Turning and turning in the widening gyre,

the falcon cannot hear the falconer;
and control is lost to the reigning avatar
bringing the stones to pile on the pyre
to smother the truth and put out the fire.
Sound the alarm! Call an amateur!
The falcon cannot hear the falconer.

Things fall apart; the center cannot hold;
new ideas gallop away to be sold
for a penny for the batch,
while little else can be matched
and nothing new is prepared as bold.
Things fall apart; the center cannot hold;

mere anarchy is loosed upon the world.
The evil thoughts come from the burled
place of government's secrets unrevealed,
hidden from view and resealed
away from the public eye like a flag furled.
Mere anarchy is loosed upon the world.

---

[9] From W. B. Yeats's "The Second Coming."

Made to Last

Let's value a poem as a pulse,
a food crop, and it is the impulse
with meaning for the rest of the lot
that gives me this thought:
more satisfying dinners of
poetry and pulses can be labors of love.

As early humans sat around their fires
eating food and discussing the day's desires,
poets burst into poetry. Strong emotional
responses to nature and their notions
yielded poetic readings in these
communities, I continue to tease.

I imagine that appropriate seasonings
for pulses with the ham hocks from a wild reason
turned any mess of peas or beans
into a hearty meal, just as means
of poetic devices turn a group of words blunted
into a pleasing poem after a successful stunt.

I maintain in this comparison that humans
hardly ever ventured beyond their native lands
without taking pulses and poetry with them,
making impulses and poems a common stem.
Take a mixture of chickpeas or any bean
and chips and lines of poems seem

like pita dipped into hummus,
making the words hum for us.
Poems shared with the plate of pork sausage
and dark red kidney beans enhance wattage
of the enjoyment and nourishment hooked
to the soul. The great northern beans cooked

down with ham, with hocks and bits of poetic
ham, slow cooked for hours aesthetic,
around the edge of the prophetic,
allow the poet to introduce more diversity
to the audience and add value to ease
the poem. Black-eyed peas in the new year

with a little salt meat consumed with poetic future
are known to bring good luck to the user.
The reading of a poem enhances the feeding
of the pulse and its history, heeding
the value of the poem and the survival
of good times with friends and rivals.

Mardi Gras Parade

Fat Tuesday is the day
of parades with many buffets.
The excitement swells with parade
goers. Hours slowly make way
for the floats for this special charade.
Gold and purple designs
appear in dress on fans,
making festive lines.
The riders call to the many hands,
throwing colored beads and bangles
to waiting eager bystanders.
Crowds sport the colors at every angle.
From the Zulu floats, coconuts
are the prizes valued by those with guts.

Morning

The sun rises in an hour from behind trees,
its rise spreading sunlight over the scene.
It glows like a bright lemon for all to see.
Sleepers awake, get ready for routine.

They are not aware of the warmth of morning
until they walk out of doors to admire
azaleas, cannas, and myrtles adorning.

Sun on high, the day like golden honey.
Drivers leave home to make money.

Nature's Law

Nothing shows beautiful
like the trunks of myrtles.
The gnarly legs shoot up
toward the clear blue sky.
Nature's laws are clear—
Nature's laws are clear,
and the limbs shed bark
until silvery pink. Surrounded
by green monkey grass,
the trunks become natural art.

Nature Welcomes Spring

Nature welcomes spring.
Trees and plants bud, dressed
yellow green, green yellow, green,
each following the secretive
internal design
until old and mature ...

The trees, listening to the wind,
march down the lanes,
their young under their limbs,
woodsy homes for helpful guests.
The birds build their homes
on the limbs, safety there.
Over the young growth
the trees keep vigil
until the tree meets destiny.

When the life of a tree ends,
the young trees thrive straight and strong
in a playground for all,
teaching their young to survive.
Skinks play along the limbs
while birds sing and squirrels work.
Nature salutes the next spring ...

New Restaurant

Her head rises up now and then
from behind the shelf that receives
the food she prepares for customers.
Seeing as she is still brave and stalwart, no one would
know the pain she has endured. From
war and carnage in Armenia
during her relatives' lives to the new home
in this country, she never imagined
the joy and the pain of living. She
and her remaining son closed
their first restaurant after
her husband and son died.
She disappeared for a year or so.
Then one day she was waving
from the door of a new restaurant
in a new location with new signage.
Her restaurant business improved,
and she was almost happy once again.

Ode to a Fork

The silver fork is a friend
to eat with. It is a comfort
to the hands and fingers.
The tongs, balanced
against weight of the handle,
facilitate easy access to food,
whether spearing or lifting.
Like another kind of fork,
it takes us on a culinary hunt
for delicious tastes. With a fork
in a road, drivers have to make
a choice. Take a right to find
a restaurant or a left to find
a new adventure. A fork
in the trunk of a tree
is not always a good thing
to have, but it does provide a heavy
load of leaves on each limb, like
a full head of lettuce. So it is
with the fork to scoop or spear truth.

On the Brink

He landed in a slump near
the back of the classroom, locked
in silence until he was comfortable
with his surroundings. When he finally
became a member of the classroom,
he flashed his intelligence and spun
his humor with all. His brashness
mellowed and he became a respected
member of the class community.
Others remained unaware
as he developed into a poet,
carving emotion into words
to fill the holes in his armor.
He reigned as the figurative delight
of the classroom and left in his place
a garden of music.

Phoenix

She has more courage
than the average person,
marrying more than once and
divorcing twice, but these trials
did not stop her from being
a good mother to two girls,
protecting them like a mountain
lioness defending her cubs.
Her blonde curls, still quite tight,
frame her resolve with commitment.
Her girls are grown now
and are the delight of her life.
She savors every visit from them
like a comfy blanket on a cool day.
She has a love of birds and animals.
She spends a great deal of her
funds feeding transient birds and deer
that visit her home. She adopted
two Weimaraners from someone
who could no longer take care
of them. The older dogs adjusted
well and became members
of the family, spoiled by both
her and her husband, who took
them on daily walks and rides
around the neighborhood.
The sudden death of one of the dogs
broke her heart and left her as empty
as a discarded cereal box, but she will
rise again like a phoenix, not from the sand
in the desert but from more
solid rock, as she always does.

Night Work

The night hovering like faceted crystals,
the moon silver-plated the trees and bushes.
The ravens to their friends sent whistles
with calls that wrecked the peace of the hushes.

No one knows their intent as the men load
the boats in secret, heading to unknown places.
The rising sweat of men on the brow shows.

The boat is full, and tired men can rest.
The secret cargo will make the high crest.

Question Mark

Curvaceous instigator of answers,
I reign. Call me out to the dance, and
I will flaunt my curves. I can turn
respectfully upside down, right or left
in the dance, and lead my partner
to a possible commitment. Agreeable,
I wait to be direct or indirect when used.
I can wait with the winds impatiently,
but I whip up from nowhere
to the unexpected. I can cause words
to soar, instill the hunt for explanations,
cause inquiry, or query for an answer.
My first use was in Syriac language (:)
to ask a question. I reappeared
in the eighth century, so I am
qualified to help out with historical data
when the proof is not available because of
missing or unknown information. I can be
used as a wildcard character, or a substitute
in modern computing. I denote a bad move
in the game of chess. I forgot to tell you—
I am quite versatile and still pretty
after all these years.

Rainy Monday

The house sleeps in complete darkness. The rain falls outside
in steady patterns as the rain spirits tap on the windows.

Only the low whirring of the computer interrupts the silence.
The glow from the screen provides only enough light for typing.

The darkness of the room feeds my sleepiness. A glass of merlot
wraps me in warmness, making a nap impossible to avoid.

I know that any sleep from wine is short. I will awake before I want to,
feeling energized and ready to exercise. How I cheat you, Morpheus!

I search the room for lines to this poem, but the room does not
draw my muse to the connecting spirit.

An hour has passed on this hopeful adventure. Apollo and Erato,
where are you? This frustration stays my inspiration.

The room lightens as the sky clears. Through the glass in the door,
I see the promise of a rainbow dividing the remaining clouds.

Rising to the Occasion

Something there is that doesn't love a wall,
That sends the frozen-ground-swell under it,
And spills the upper boulders to the sun;
And makes gaps even two can pass abreast.[10]

Something there is that doesn't love a wall,
as with a weed or grass that ignores the stall
in its growth, entwines its blades and stems
and pushes up between and from under the whims
of those who try to destroy Nature's call.
Something there is that doesn't love a wall

that sends the frozen groundswell under it.
As all gains ground and grows fit,
we become more annoyed and barge
in with damaging weapons in the charge.
The ground will grow richer from weeds' spit
that sends the frozen groundswell under it

and spills the upper boulders to the sun,
a special happening that fascinates none.
Thinking more about the tolerance of my friends
and more about the rightful place for their blend,
and in a new spirit I become a nation of one
and spill the upper boulders to the sun.

And I make gaps even two can pass abreast
that complement the nation of no needless arrests.
Let's become known as the defender of our sisters and brothers.
Let no one find himself or herself as an "other"
or find oneself subjected to arrest,
and make gaps even two can pass abreast.

---

[10] From Robert Frost's "Mending Wall."

Samantha

Such a mighty name
that was kept meek
by the whining
of her fifties Pontiac.
Its whine always
announced her as she
pulled into the driveway,
bouncing and bumping
to a stop. Her visit would
include the complaints
of a princess who had
not received her just
pampering. She knew
the rules and applied
them to her life. She
knew what was good
for everyone, whether
she liked them or not.
But the taste of her baking,
especially her apple pie,
always kept the delight
in her visits.

Bluebird Shelter for Squirrels

Sightings of tornado funnels flooded
the television screen all morning. Outside
the rain fell steady. Weary of watching TV,
I went to the window for some relief,
only to see two squirrels scurry for shelter
from the rain into a bluebird house
close to the main house. They had gnawed
the soft cedarwood hole larger at an earlier time
because it was large enough for them to slip through.
One stuck his head out of the hole
in the birdhouse as if to keep watch
on the weather. The look on his face
showed he was just as concerned
about the weather as I was.

Sherman

He was a tall, thin man with a tuft
of hair that hung over his forehead,
known throughout the parish
and the surrounding parishes
as a fun-loving person. Being born
deaf did not keep him
from developing friendships
and making good friends.
His steely blue eyes would break
into a smile, and he would come quickly
to give a hug or shake a hand. He loved
to tease about anything and everything, and
he would gesture until the friend got the joke.
His delight at seeing other people
he knew never grew tiring for him,
not even when he was dying. He was
beloved by the community, and
his absence was felt by all.

The Sight of Trees

The leaves of the trees
form a large crown of green.
Their limbs reach down as if to touch,
balancing their limbs from their trunks.
Their roots entwine beneath them
the way human arms
wrap around each other.
They take care of and feed
the sick of their own kind,
and harbor helpful guests
much the way we do.
I find myself thinking
that I am walking
among the seeing
when I walk under the trees
and feel them gawking.
Using cell bodies as a lens with ease,
they focus on the image of the last source
with a cell structure much the way
the retina of the human eye does.
The warmth of trees has always
soothed me, and I feel comforted
in their presence. Shall we
look forward to the scientific day
when we photograph plant cells
acting like lenses and we learn
in the end which plants put
their rudimentary sight out to spin?

Silently It Came

We went to bed hoping and expecting.
When we awoke the next morning,
the snow had silently covered
the roofs of houses nearby and
the bushes and trees. The blanket of
snow hung like whipped crème
on the limbs of the azaleas, chrysanthemums,
and crepe myrtles. In the afternoon,
the blanket of whipped crème moved
to the feet of the bushes and trees. Only
a small plop of snow remained
on the leaves. Silently it came, and
it disappeared just as silently, in 2017.

Sounds of Thunder

When the thunder rumbles and threatens rain,
sounds of rumbling echo through the dark sky
and the sounds linger ... as the storm gains
distance and leaves the night by and by.

The quietness appears now frozen
as if collected and slipped
into the night. The rumbles can
barely be heard in the far distance.

The night is still young—conversation time.
I find my favorite recipe
while friends look for board games
when the thunder rumbles and threatens rain—

In the House

The car rolled to the gate of the short driveway.
The moonlight hung like a bright lemon over the house.
The stars smiled and winked in full sight,
no clouds in the clear sky. Inside, the house was very dark
except for the moonlight shining through the windows—
filling the dark rooms with grief for the missing in the deserted house.

The darkness gobbled up every speck of light in the house.
It was hard to move in pitch-black, often stumbling to find my way.
Moonlight crept in only at the windows,
and shards blocked by furniture bounced around the house
when the light tiptoed through the rooms of darkness.
Candles burning low flashed and dripped but provided little sight.

As my eyes adjusted to the candlelight,
I began the search for the documents hidden in the house.
The task started in her bedroom, still dark.
Dresser on the left, bed in the middle, chest in sight—
this stop was the first from the back door of the house.
If only she were here, I would not be using moonlight.

Sitting down on her bed for comfort in front of the window,
I paused, thinking about her last time home and this sight.
The breakfasts of sausage and eggs in the house
stalled the search for a moment before I walked again through the house.
The papers should be in the first drawer. Then I can be on my way.
The rooms felt like deep caves as I tried to see into them in the dark.

When daybreak comes, will I be more lucky than I am in the dark?
It took longer than I thought with only moonlight through the window.
I made it through the house again to see my car safe in the driveway.
As I made my way back to the bedroom without candlelight for sight,
I returned to the first drawer of the chest in her bedroom in the house,
keeping memories of her at bay so I could complete the search.

I pulled open the drawer in her bedroom of the house.
I was surprised that the drawer was so dark.
I could see nothing! The drawer loomed dark like the rest of the house.
Flashlight! The weak moonlight was not enough from the window.
My hand shook as I looked—I slipped down on the bed to rest my sight.
There it was in front of me—I could not see anything now in the way.

I fell across the bed and slept crossways, dreaming of my years in the house.
What a sight! The darkness replaced by the sunshine through the windows—
I awoke suddenly more contented, and the deserted house seemed more alive.

Spinning It

Library space fills.
Young poets in one row,
seated together, quiet.
The reading begins soon.
Student poet reads poem—
Student poet reads poem
stirring inspiration
that fills the guest poet
and the group with delight.
Praise equals the applause.

Starlight

At Van Gogh's *Starry Night*
I stand beside the old
tree trunk and look down on
the village below, the
blue sky bursting with stars.
Blue sky bursting with stars,
the game begins soon.
Supporters of teams
fill the bleachers early—
a night of smiles and joy.

Summer Morning

Uncombed hair, blurry eyes,
I stumble to the light.
I feed the patient cat
and wait for the newspaper.
Favorite songs cascade—
Favorite songs cascade
from the walls in the room,
rhythms that make me want to dance.
I cannot resist—then I realize
there's only warm air from the vents.

Survivor

As with a lot of young men
in this small town, he found
the opportunities of employment
few and so he joined the military.
Much to his favor, he was selected
to be part of the Honor Guard
at the White House. After finishing
his tour, he took courses and earned
a master's degree. He married
and had a son. As he worked
hard, he landed a job as a guard
in a federal prison, which he came
to enjoy until the day he walked down
the hallway to meet his attacker.
Stabbed twenty times but fighting
off the assailant, he was rescued
by quick-thinking guards
arriving to halt the attack. The
recovery has been slow over
the years, but he survives
to make his way again.

The Aggressor

It was a mild day
without much wind.
The sun was bright.
I noticed a blackbird
on a pole close by.
With one fell swoop,
a sparrow landed beside
the large bird. As if he
knew that it would work,
the sparrow pecked
the blackbird squarely
on his side. The blackbird
gave ground and landed
a little farther away. But
for an aggressive sparrow,
this move presented a bigger
problem. He cascaded over to
the new resting place of
the blackbird and gave
him several more pecks.
The blackbird continued
to ignore the aggressor,
but flew farther away.
The sparrow returned
to the first pole as if
to say that he had done
his duty for family
and country.

The Beginning

I sat listening,
watching,
studying
his soft blue eyes,
his smile,
and his slim, tanned fingers
as they played
with the napkin.
This college student had
approached me earlier
that morning after class.
Making conversation,
he told of his
tour of duty with the Navy.
There in a twenty-minute break
between classes
was the beginning.

The Gully

We drove the truck along the property lines
to check for downed fences that allowed
the cattle to stray over to the neighbors'.
Luckily for us, there were no downed fences.
I asked about the gully, but no one seemed
to remember it. I declared that it was on

the property, but clearer minds said it was not.
As the truck bounced and strained to roll over
the terraces that stopped erosion, I yearned to get
out to find the gully I held in my memory.
It was there as I knew it through the trees
and a short walk to the fence line.

I remembered playing cowboys and Indians
along the deep red clay sides. Galloping up
the steep sides a piece and deep into the ravine,
we spent hours amusing ourselves, resting
at the bottom when too tired to move. It was
hard to climb the steep sides back up to the top.

I thought it was located at the far end of the family land.
No one seemed to care about it, and no one
was interested in visiting and exploring.
Suddenly, the large mouth of earth opened
wide and deep, revealing red clay sides and bottom.
There it was! At the middle edge of the family land.

I thought it beautiful and wondered at its mysteries
and bathed in the memories now floating over me.
The sides of the ravine were hard, and bare
of any growth after all these years in this large
valley, a landform created by running water
as if cut with a knife into the soil on this small hillside.

Only one thing was different. Now a fence
separated it from the property, and it was not
on the family property. It was now claimed
by a timber company, and exploring it was
out of the question. What a disappointment!
No rewinding future revisions of this memory!

The Eclipse on August 21

The first total eclipse in ninety-nine years, the moon passed across the country, west to east, to greet the sun. At 1:29 the two met, but the eclipse was partial here in Louisiana. This astronomical wonder ended at 2:52 p.m. There was no rain, but the beautiful fluffy clouds against the blue sky often kept the eclipse from being seen. There were libraries and other spots around town for viewers to see the eclipse. The college provided eclipse glasses for students, faculty, and staff at the parade grounds. The Art and Science Museum had a solar viewing telescope available, as well as several other indirect-viewing telescopes. Space Grant Consortium launched two high-altitude balloons to live stream aerial footage of the moon's shadow. Viewers became reflective of their religious beliefs. It was a day of celebration and comfort after seeing the eclipse.

moon moved across sun
leaving half ring of fire
that inspired all

Sun's Patina

The sun painted a golden patina
in the late evening. The day came
to a close and I moved from the arena.
Dusk settled in and covered the sum.

The restlessness stayed with me.
My attempts to write were just
attempts. I had nothing to show.
The muse had forsaken the day.

I sat and rewound my memories.
I had plenty to remember for sure,
but I thought only about the beauty
of the golden patina left by the sun.

The Visit

The morning coolness from the heavy
condensation that collects close to the earth
in the early-morning hours felt good.
The young child followed her grandpa
from the dining room to the long side porch
and down the steep steps. Both steadied
themselves by holding on to the railings
as they reached the ground. From the bottom
of the steps, the child could see the old
home site on the adjoining property
covered with oaks and hickory, where
he would indulge her fantasies and games
on days when he was up to walking about
and answering questions. From the old
weathered tool shed to down and around
the henhouse, the honeysuckle grew
thick on the fence and surrounded
the garden with its sweet smell. A few steps
more and they were standing in his small
garden. The strawberries were ripening
on a bed of pine straw. "Why do you use
pine straw?" she asked as she looked
closer at the mat of straw. He replied,
"To protect the berries and keep them clean."
"Will they be ripe soon? When I come back
to see you?" she asked.

Through the Pain

Gratitude
disarms the young ones,
giving the bearer away.

Warm feelings
fill the recipient
with comfort and happiness.

Comfort comes
from those who do care,
sharing their own good fortune.

Nothing soothes
like pure generosity,
leaving the receiver stunned.

Small favors elicit goodness,
sharing the joy through the pain.

To the Dialogue

The walk through a local art gallery
in early evening revealed the Japanese
influence of simplicity. But the show became,
instead, an evening of complexity
in the dialogue of the asymmetrical
balance of line, flat color, and pattern.
The artist's thoughts became visual:
the dialogue revealed between
the artist's creation and the art lover
was much like the beauty and the simplicity
revealed in the haiku that captures
meaning in three lines of thought.
In a mental whirlwind of understanding,
colors melded in a simplicity
that pleased.

Trip Home

The road trip begins early in the morning before the sun has greeted Earth.
Once the drive takes us off the interstate and heads us toward Mississippi next to
Louisiana, the sun is beaming through the car windows. Sun-blocking shades on
windows are placed to keep the sunrays at bay. The nearby state shows hills and
piney woods everywhere. A few houses punctuate the green of trees and grass.

sun-blocking shade
keeps away sunburn on face
no freckles on cheeks

The drive now lands us in Natchez, where the restaurants' dishes are good and
waiters welcoming. It is time to stop with the crepe myrtles blooming everywhere
and the big oaks spreading their limbs out to provide shade for the parked cars
and visitors. The walk along the brick-laden walkway takes me back to the days
of the Old South. The restaurant's door stands before us. We are greeted and
then seated by a paned window in the middle of the restaurant.

old plantation house
the structure still stands in white
a restaurant now

From the restaurant to the highway home, the oaks are massive and overhang
the roadway. A short piece to drive through the city and we cross the Mississippi
River and head back into Louisiana. The drive takes us through many small
villages of low employment and poverty. It reminds one of a third world country
with no new economic development. These small communities are dying as their
inhabitants move to the larger cities.

the wrecked cars near
the wooden houses remain quiet
no money for new

In nearly three and a half hours, the drive is closer to the old home place.
As we drive into the circle driveway of the home place, we stop and get out.
The house is still white but is in need of a paint job and repair. The bottom

boards on the sides of the house need to be replaced. The new owners have painted the inside of the house and put down a wood-resembling tile. Their decorating is minimalist and recognizable. They seem happy in the house.

where the sweet gum stood
a climbing challenge for all
the playful games no more

Watermelon Season

The terraces run the width
of the acreage. On top grow
the watermelon vines
blooming yellow on a bed
of green. The sun
is high and the rays
beat down on all.

Expectations are high
for the farmer. The first
plug of a watermelon
to determine its mellowness
is the first act to determine
when the crop will be
ready to eat. What pride
the farmer feels in the crop!

Many crops do not produce
as expected, mostly because
of nature. The more disturbing
reason: watermelons ruined—
all the melons having been plugged
by rowdy teenagers in the town.

Whip-Poor-Will's Song

When the whip-poor-will sings in the distance,
its song brightens the evening and calls forth
memories ... as I feel the coming trance,
comforted completely, northeast by north.

From the depths of the night the song
floats softly through the acres of thickets
on the breezes through the open windows.
I sit up to enable my ears to hear ...

As I listen to the bird's song, I hear
distinctly, "Chip fell out of the white oak ..."
I know that the caretaker of Nature's sounds is gone
when the whip-poor-will sings in the distance—

Windstorm

Wind howling, trees bending,
threatening my safe house,
I wind the shutters closed
to protect the windows.
Let me relax awhile—
Let me relax awhile
as I read poetry
and sip a cup of tea.
Snap! The loud crashing
sound signals a large limb falling.

The Promise of the Border

The sun rises slowly in full view.
The girl reasons that nothing bad
could happen that would clue
with what she has seen. She wonders
about leaving her remaining family.
How she loves those left behind!
She had not told anyone she was
crossing the border. She knew
of the dangers of rape or
being killed. Still she had to wake
the chance to find a better space
to live away from gang killings
and escape starvation from having
no pesos. She dreamed of sleeping
without safekeeping. She dreamed
of having plenty to eat. She could
see the train she had the ticket for,
moving nearer. As she positioned
herself to board, someone was urging
her to climb onto the top of the train.
She resisted, but the push of bodies
was impossible to resist. Suddenly,
she had to make a decision. She
went with the surge of bodies, climbing
on top of the train. On top she
felt a tense fear of what would
happen to her. She asked a friendly
face, and he said he would help her
get off the top and get where she
needed to be. Before they crossed

the border, the friendly face told
her they would get off the train.
He told her that it would not be hard
to get across the border and find
the reward of a life where she
could live and work in a free frame of mind.

Sunbathing

Twelve miles from the city,
the Atlantic Ocean billowed up
to the beach. The pillows
of waves with their whitecaps
wet the deserted beach. The sand
was so white, white as sugar, before
the water turned the sand light brown.
And the fresh smell of the waves quelled
and welcomed me. Since the depth
of the water and the current were
not known, sunbathing was the goal.
My terrier sat at the back of the beach
in the grass, letting the wind blow his ears back,
enjoying the breeze. Before long,
the waves grew bigger and washed
the beach, waking me from my short nap.

Printed in the United States
By Bookmasters